THIS BOOK BELONGS TO

____

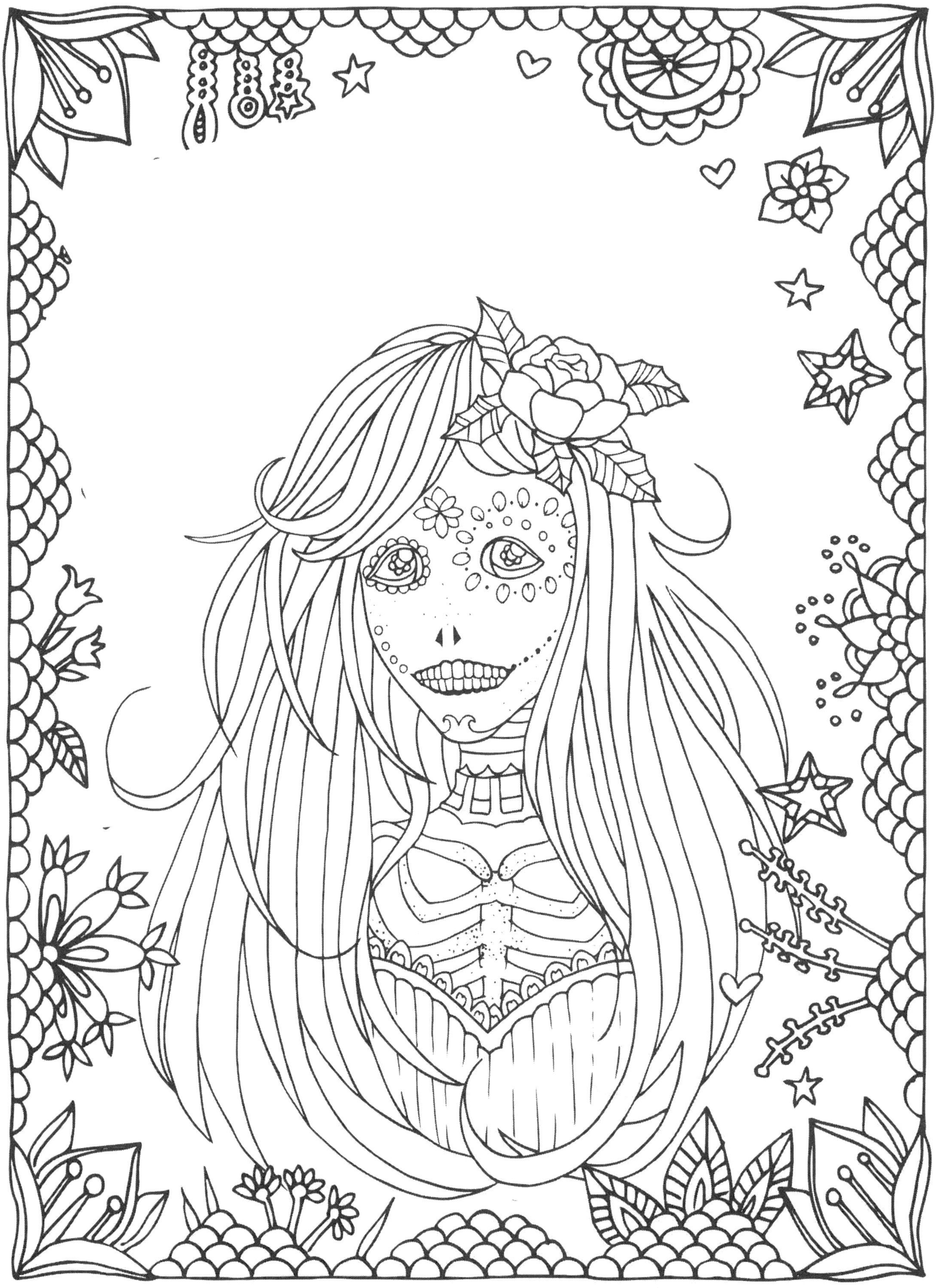

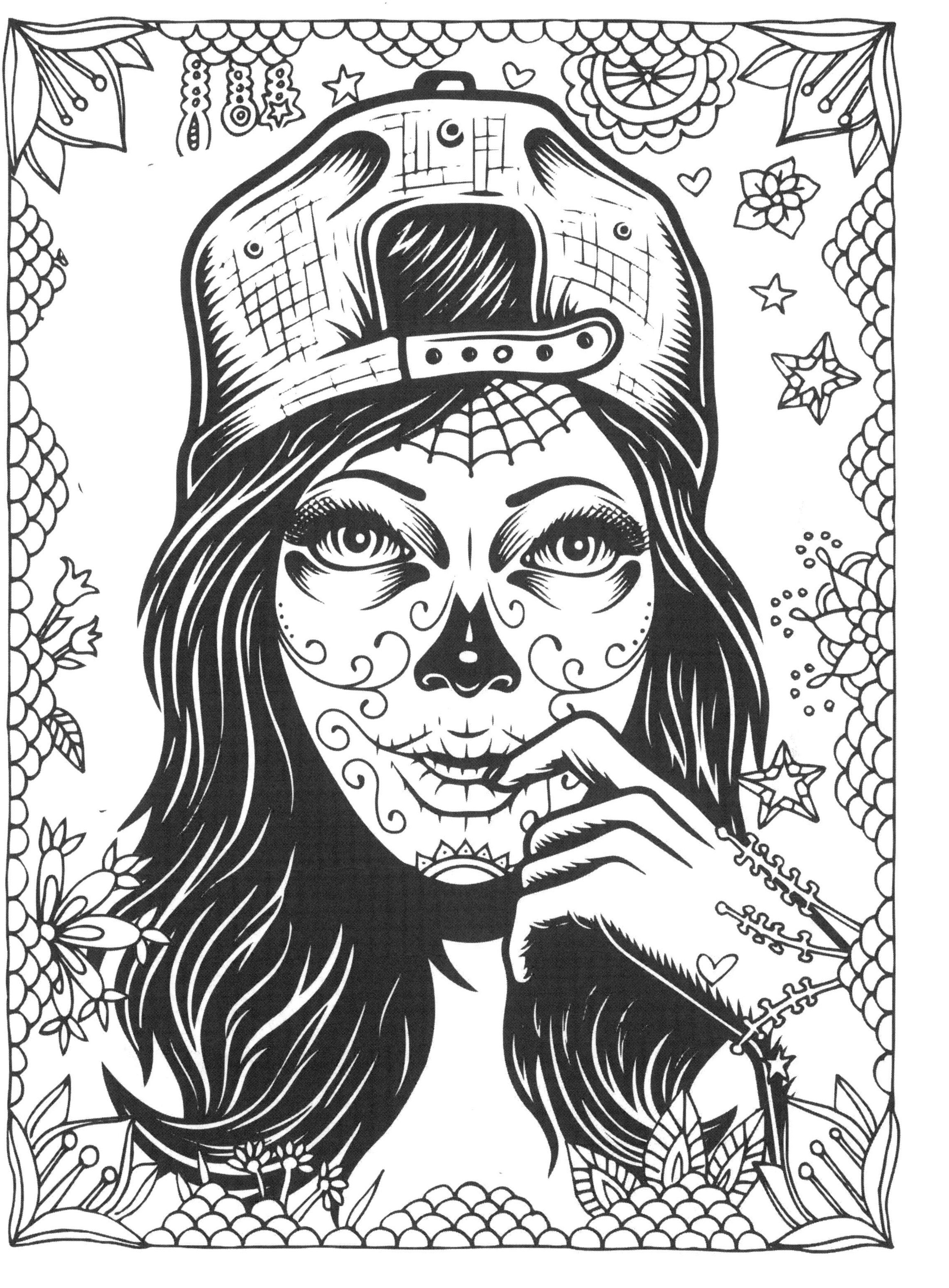

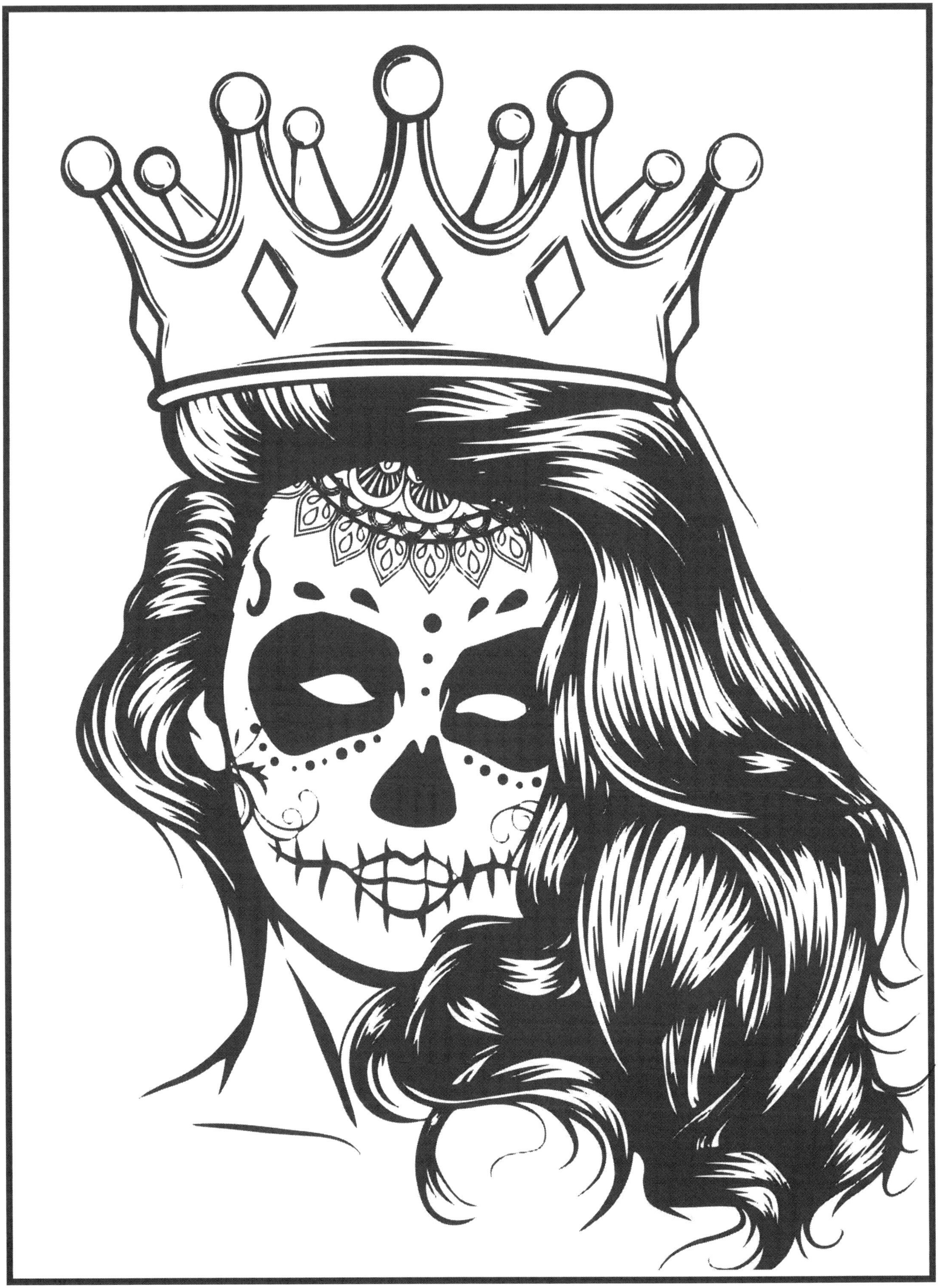

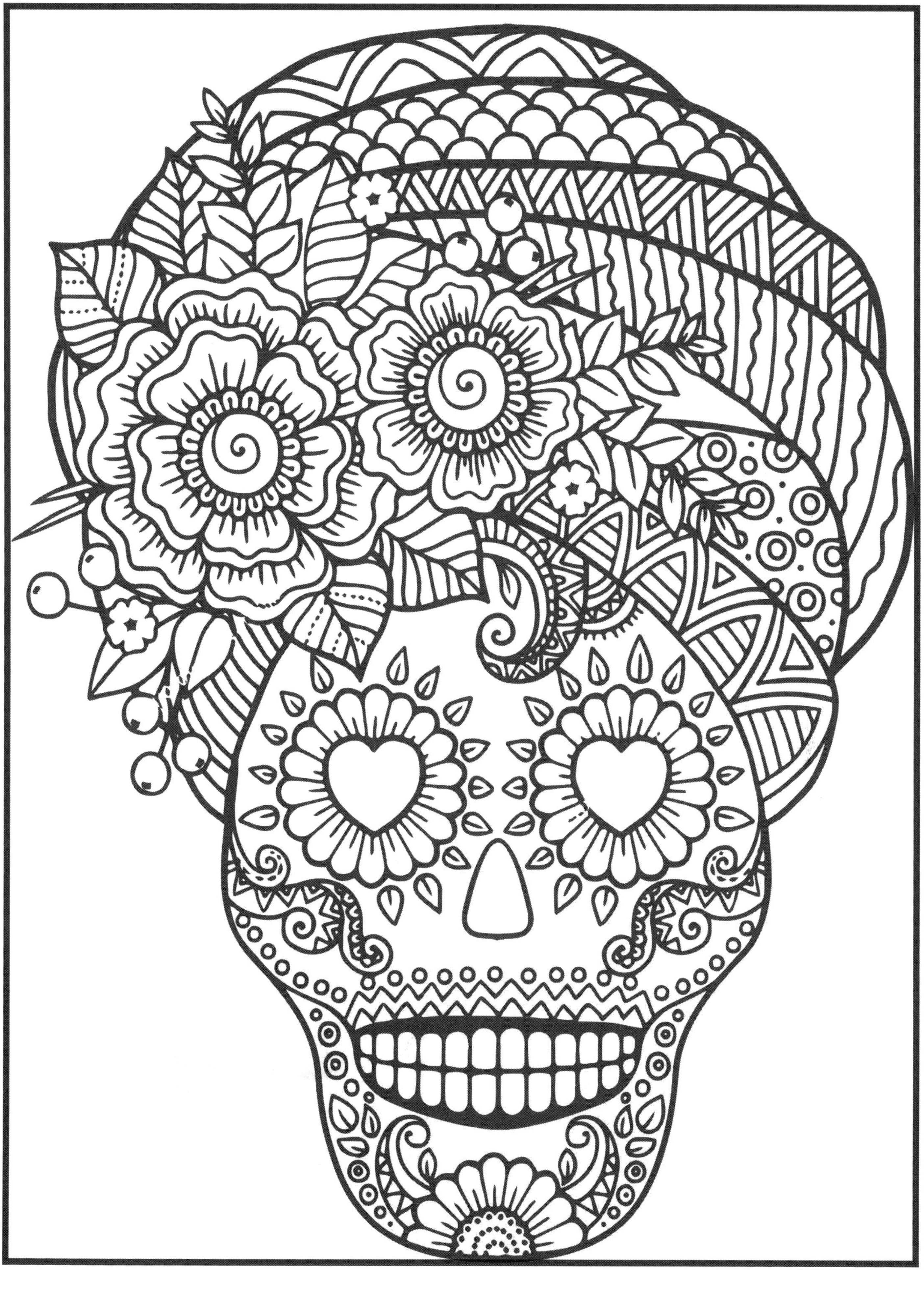

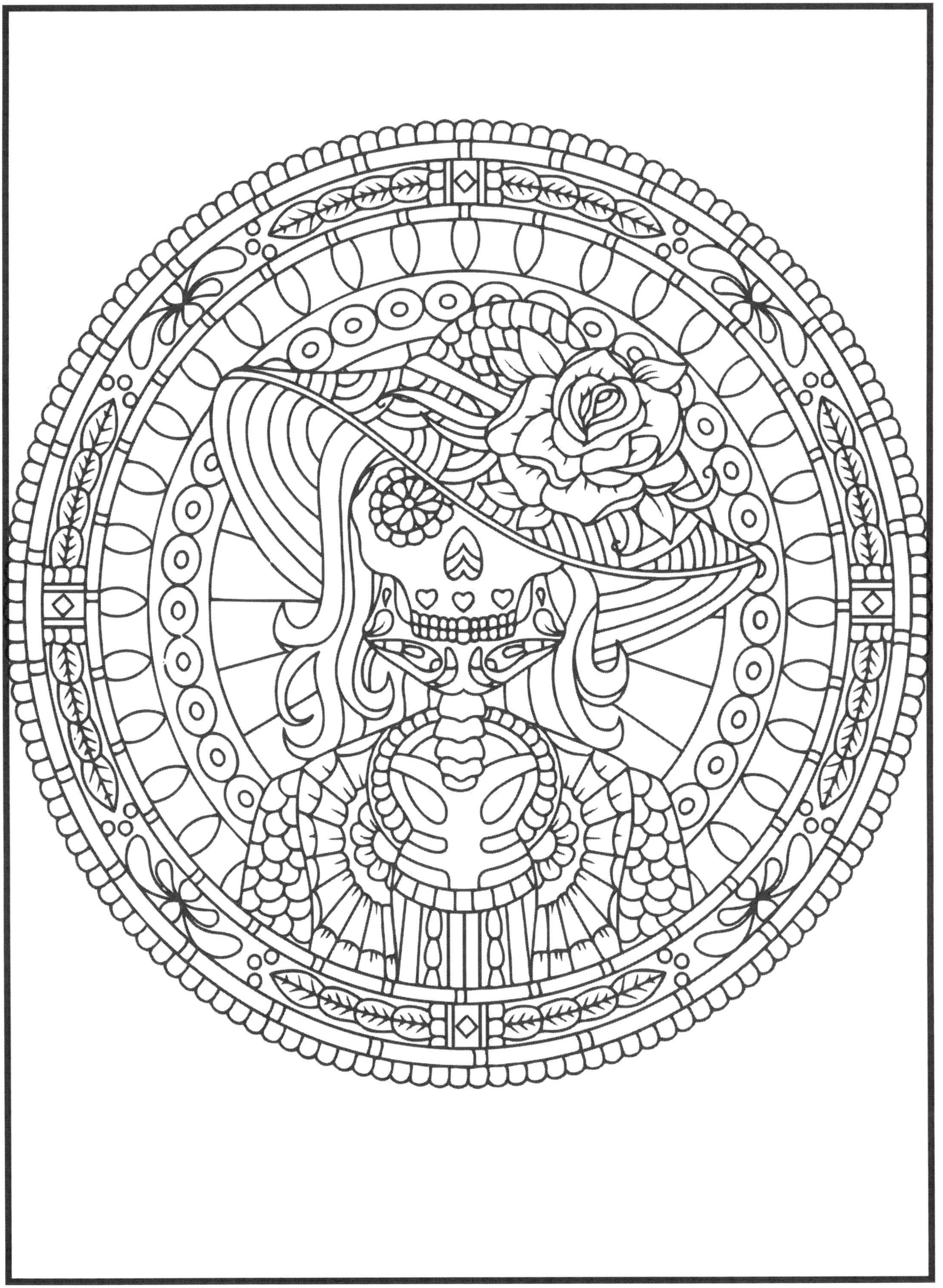

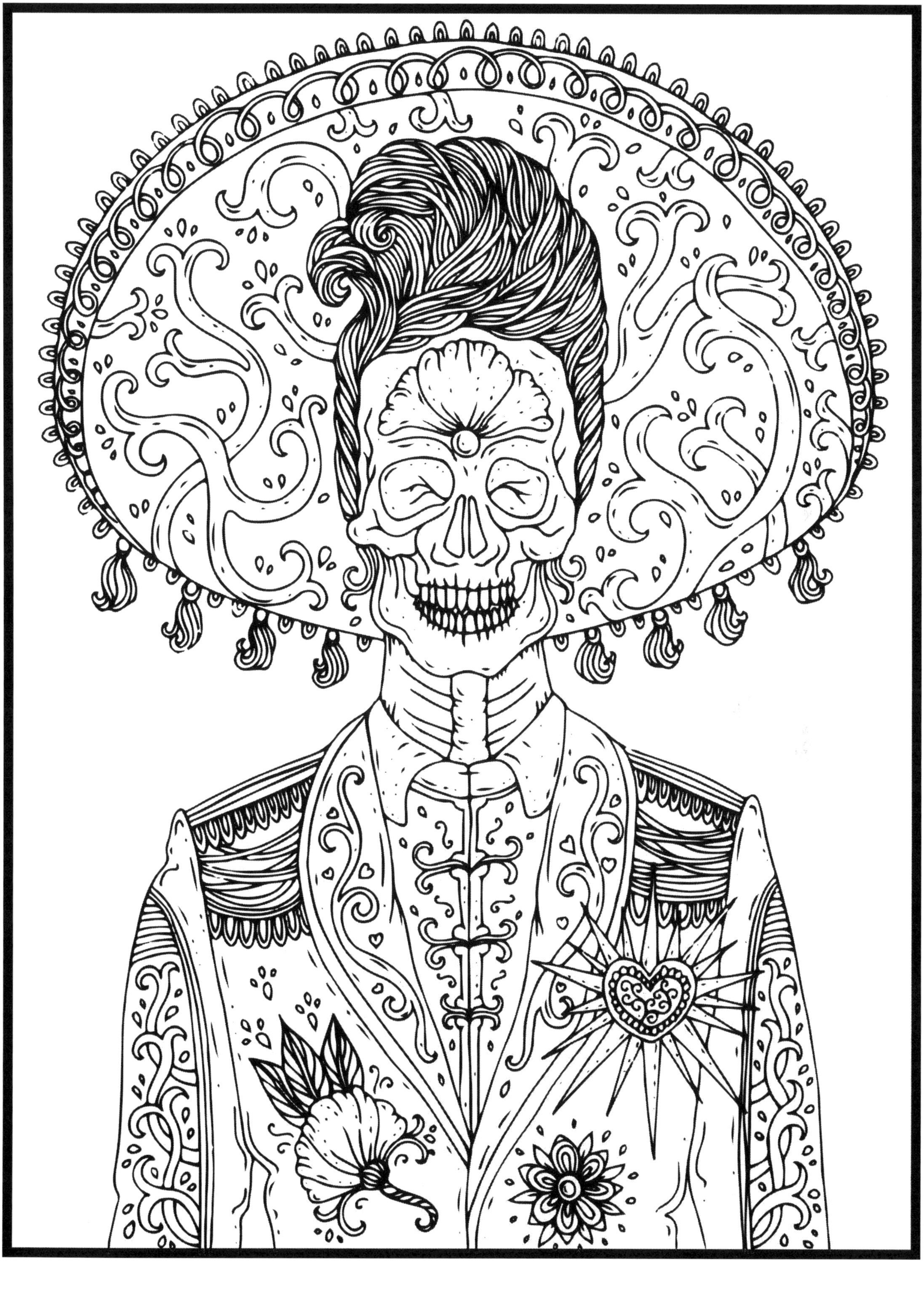

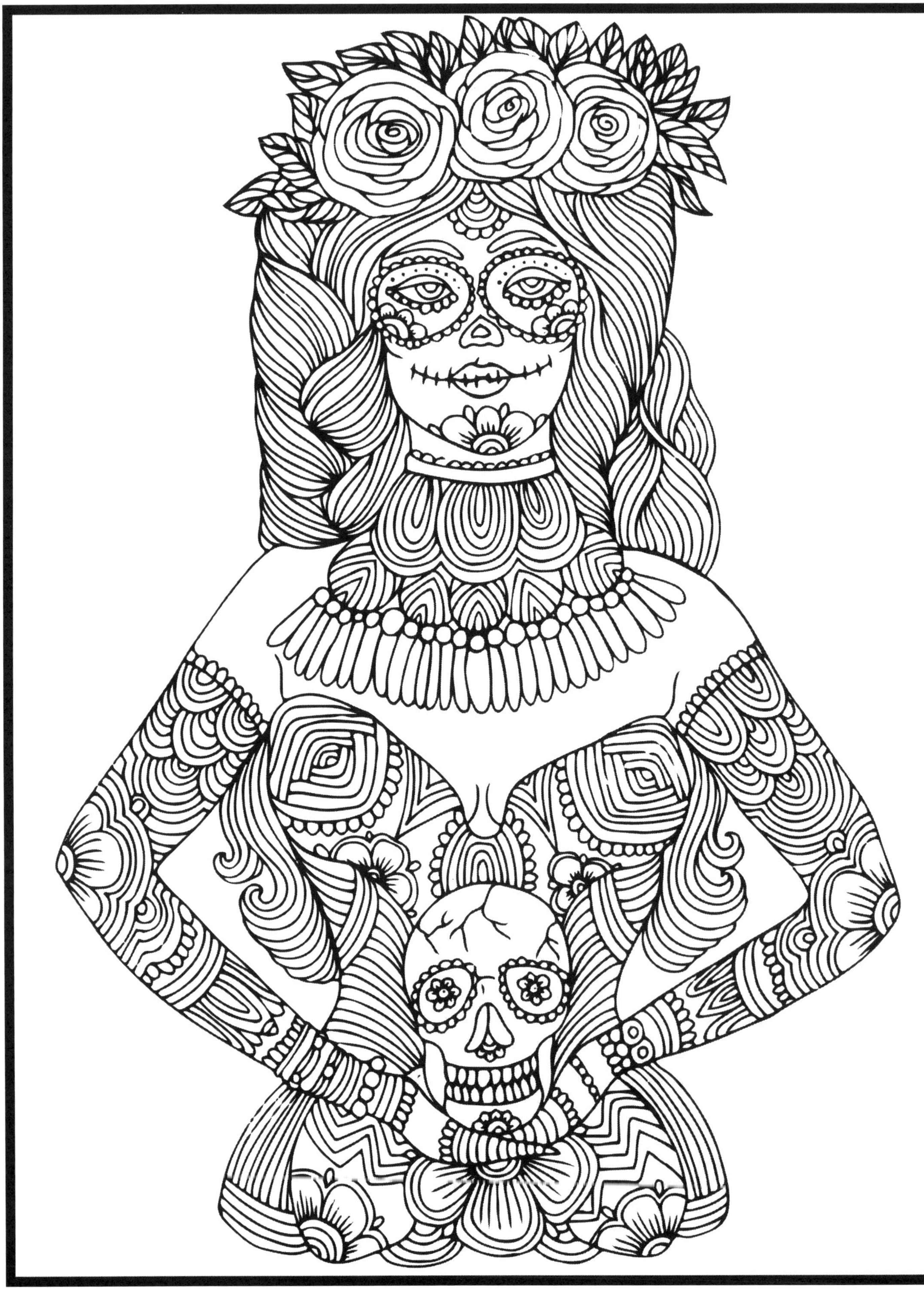

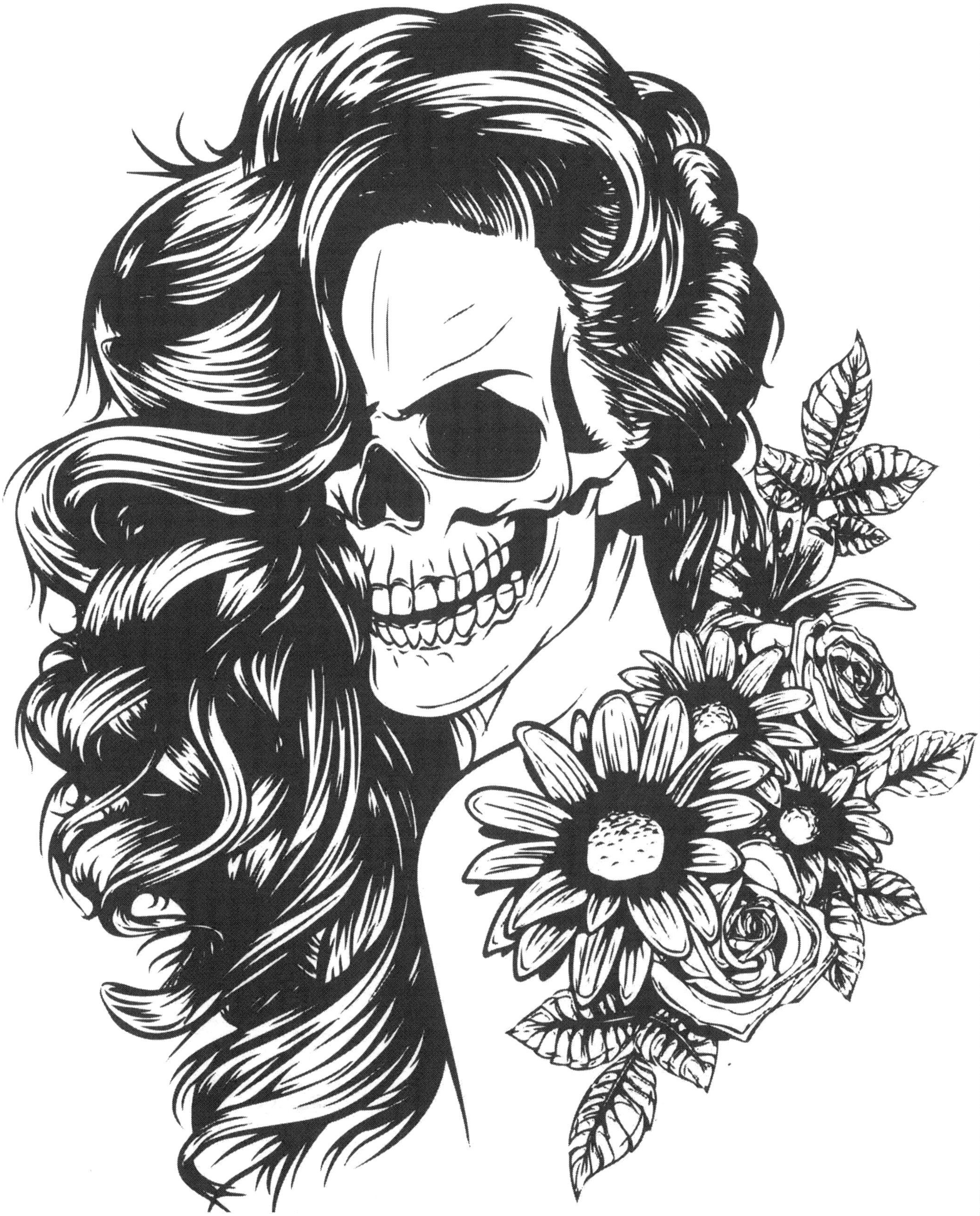

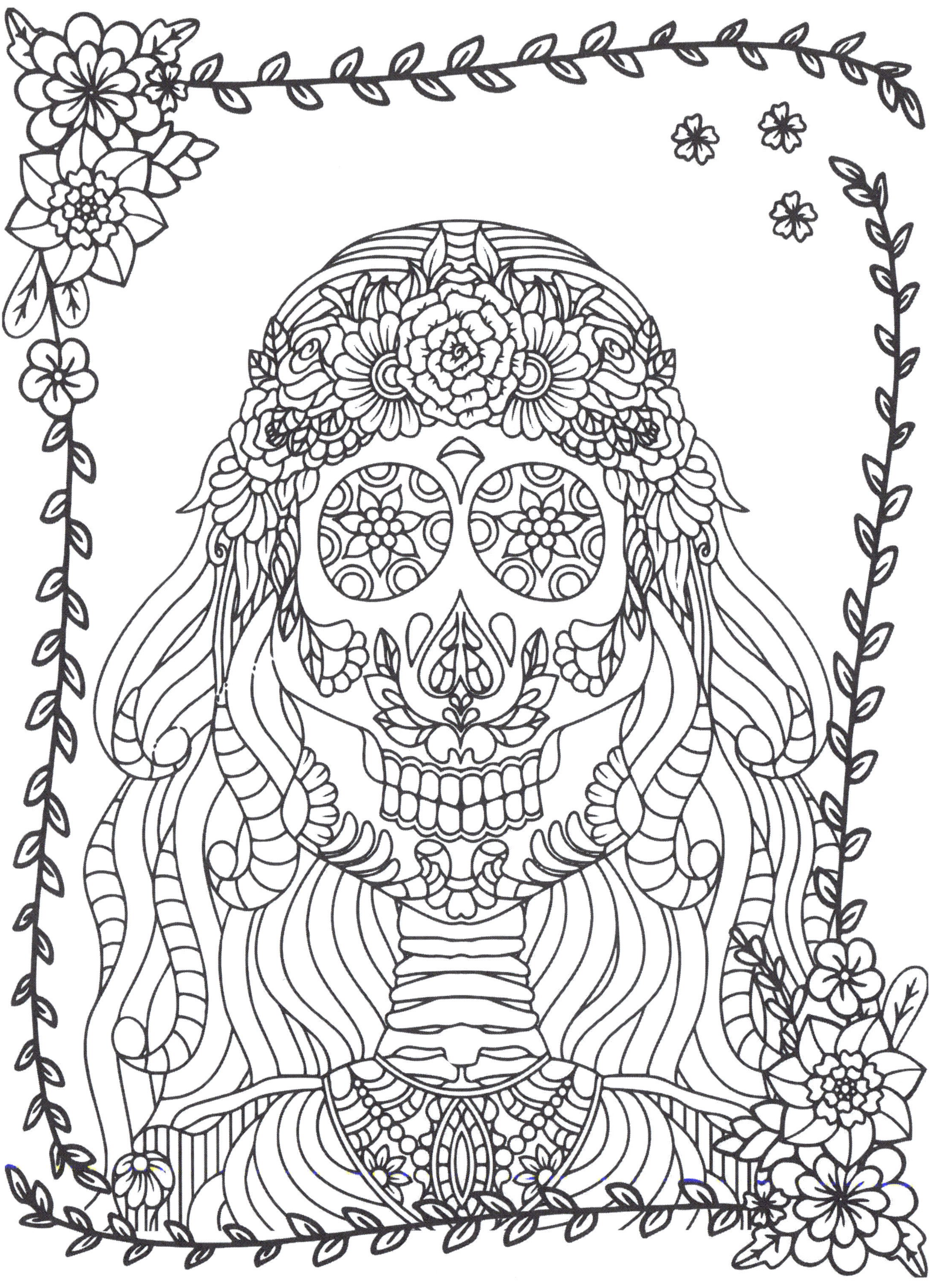

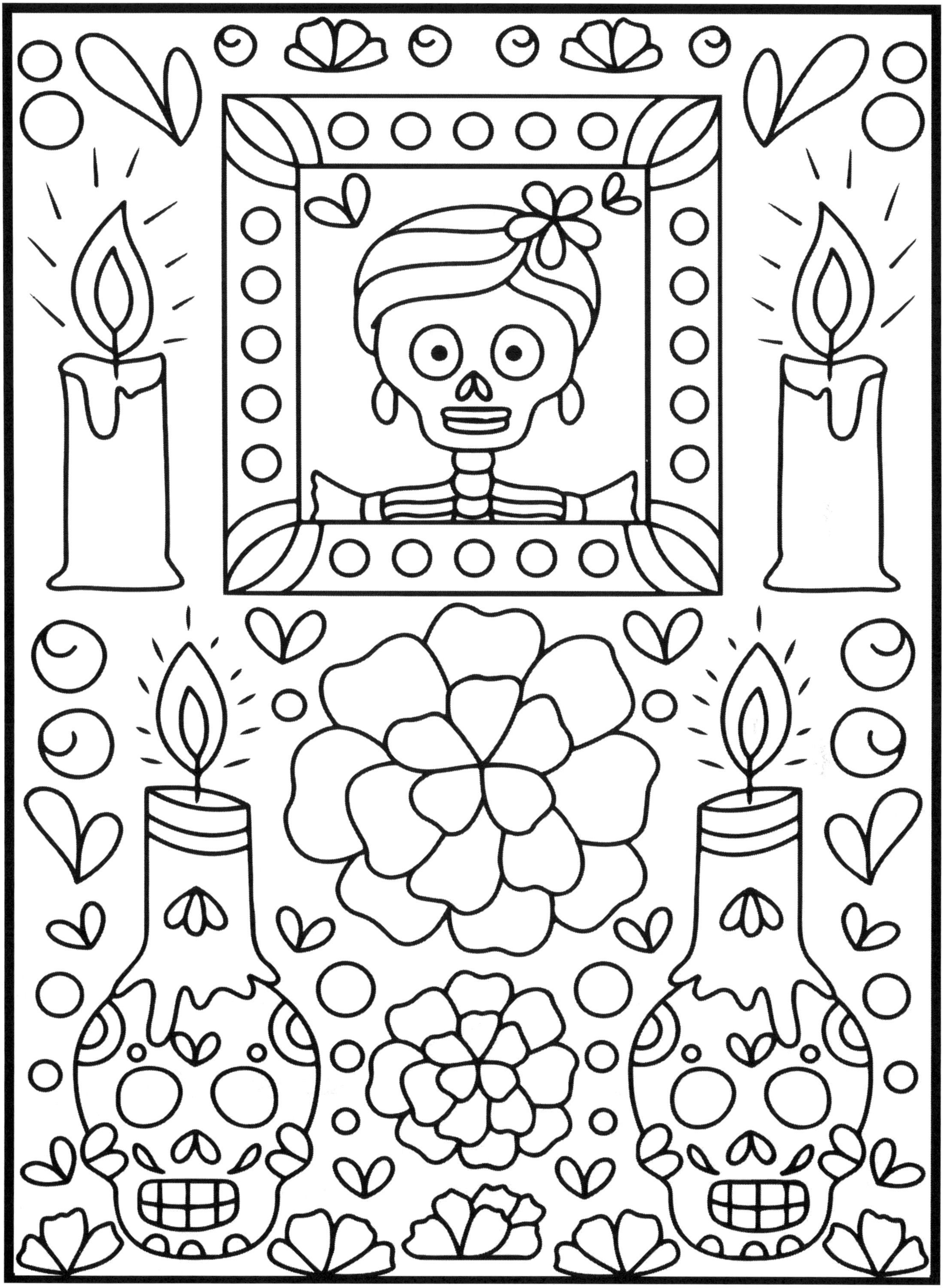

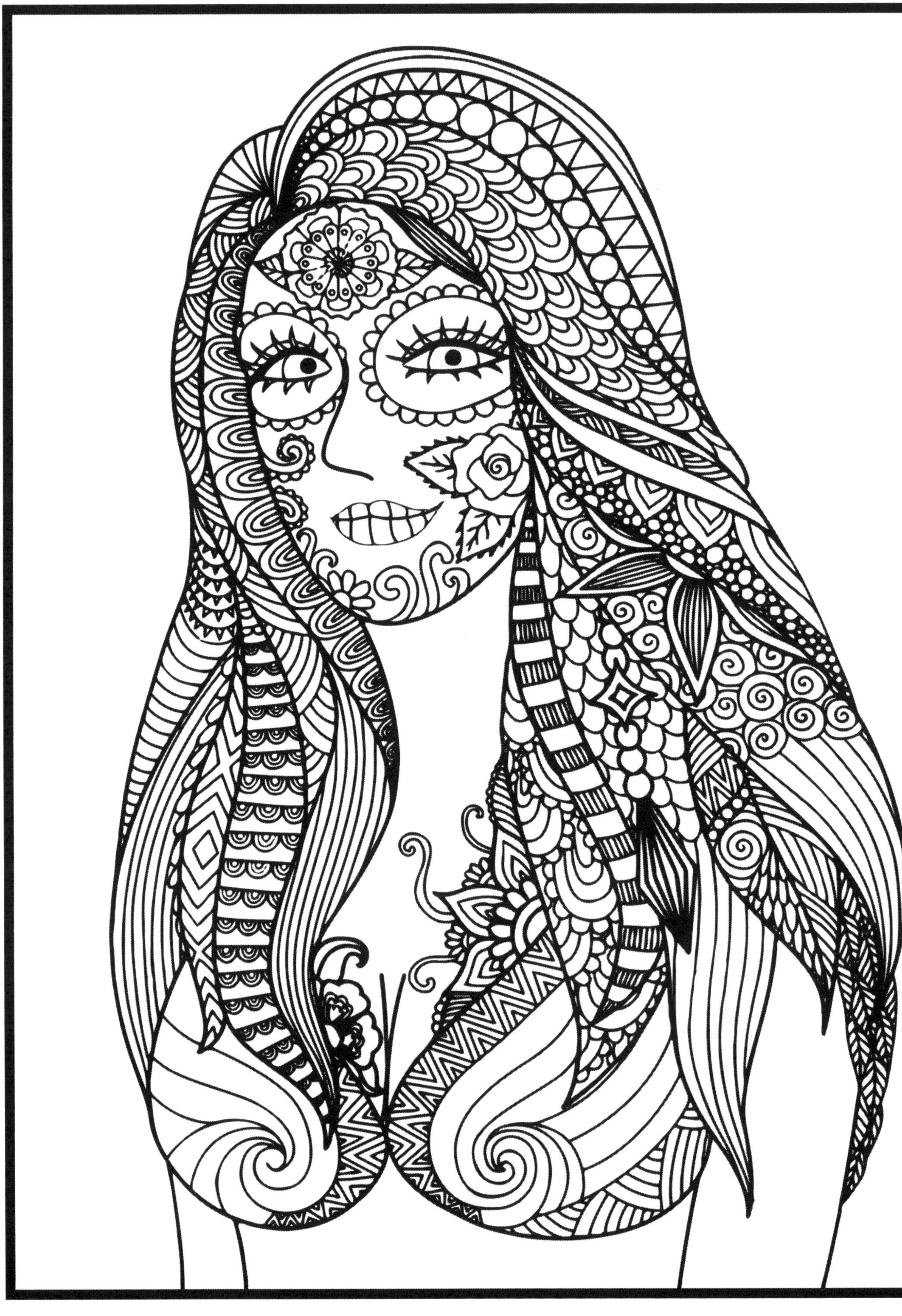

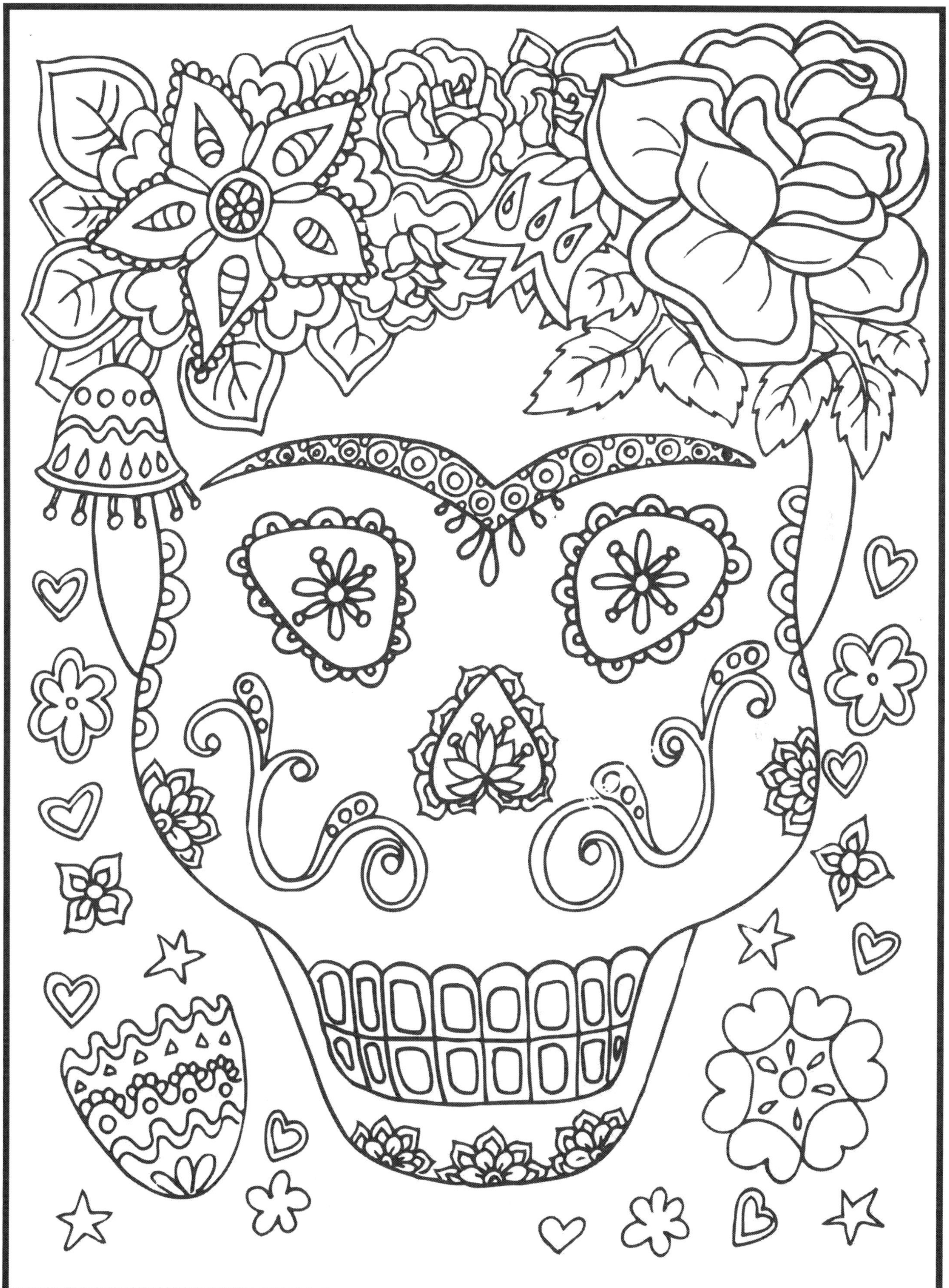

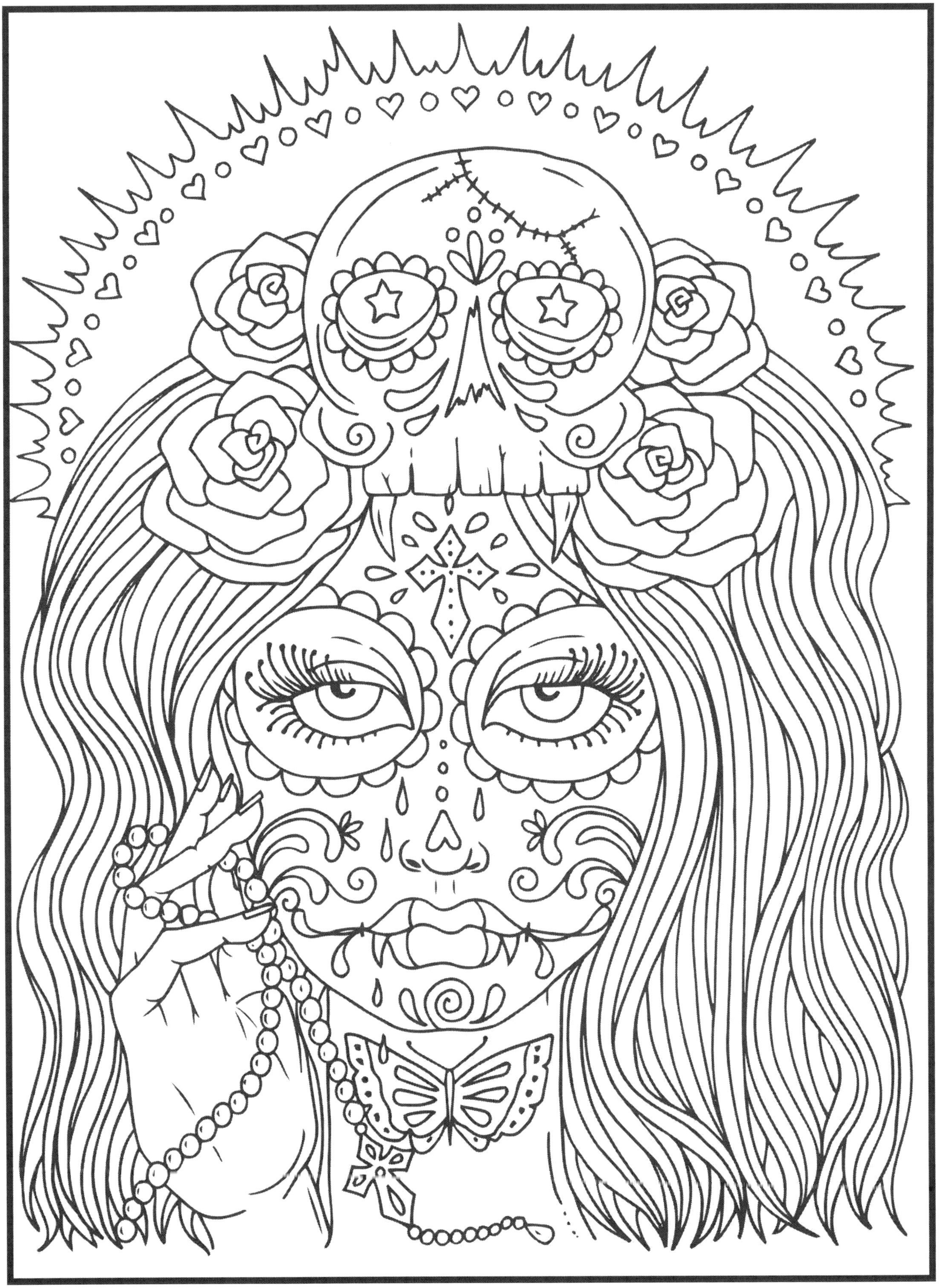

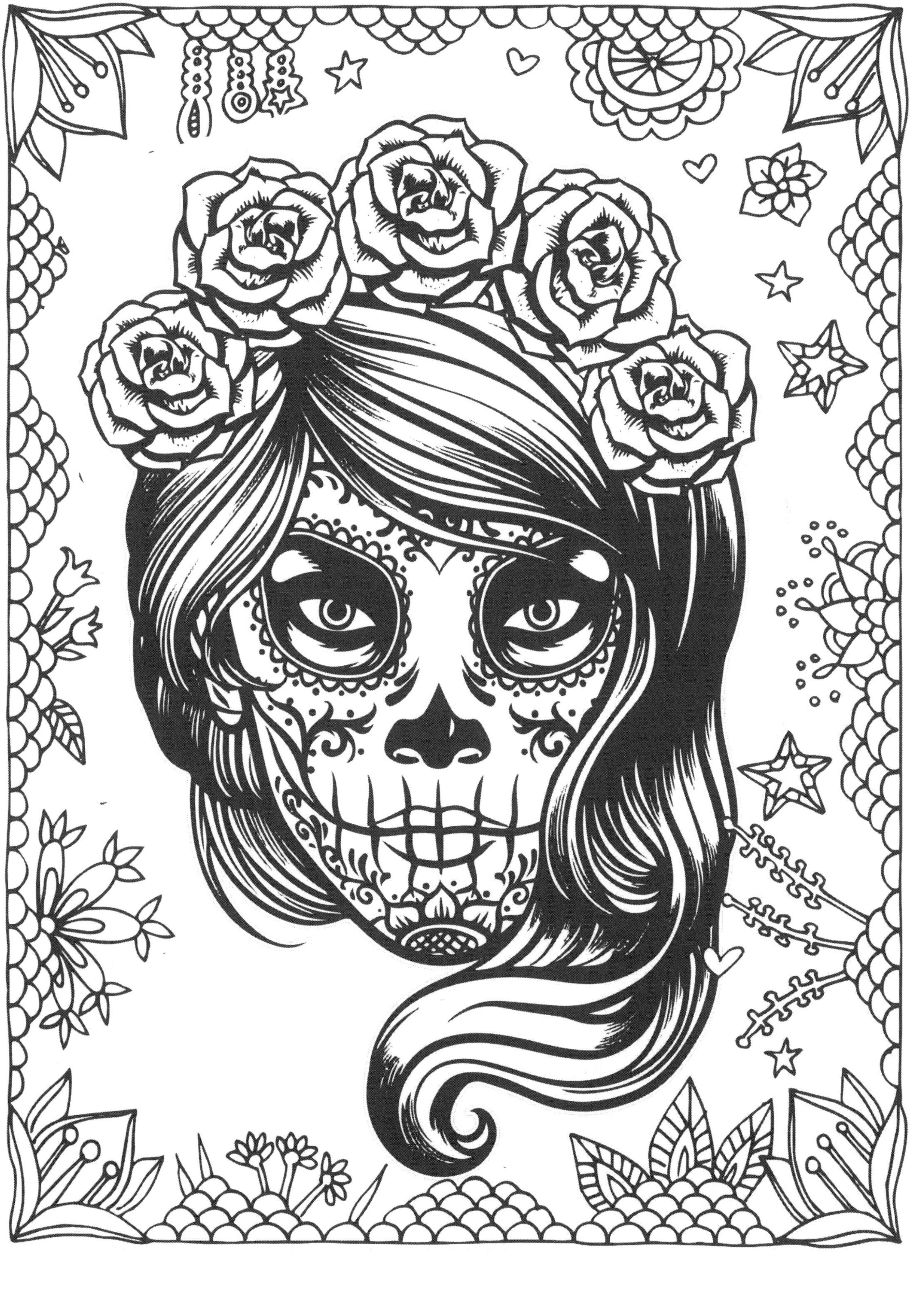

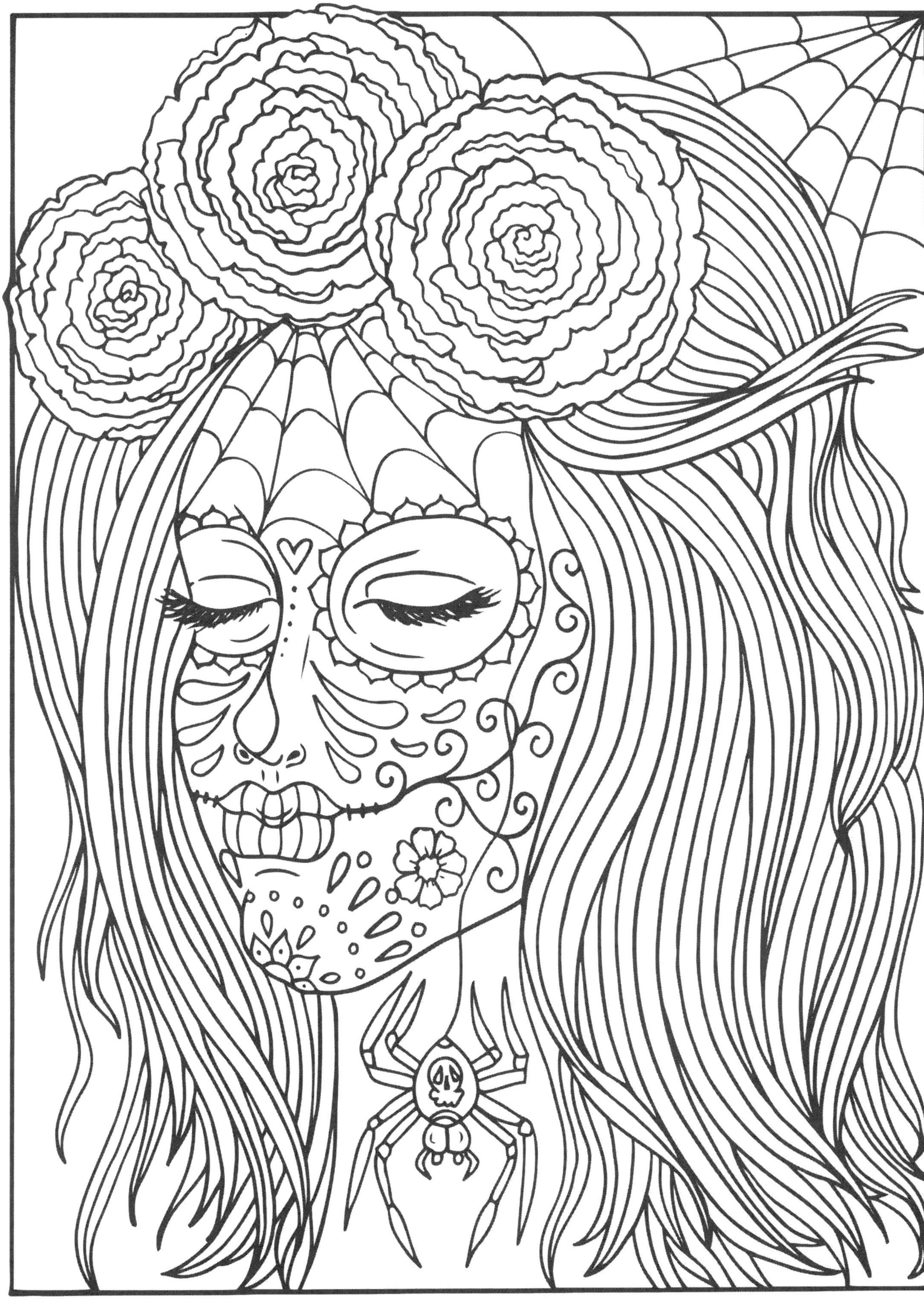

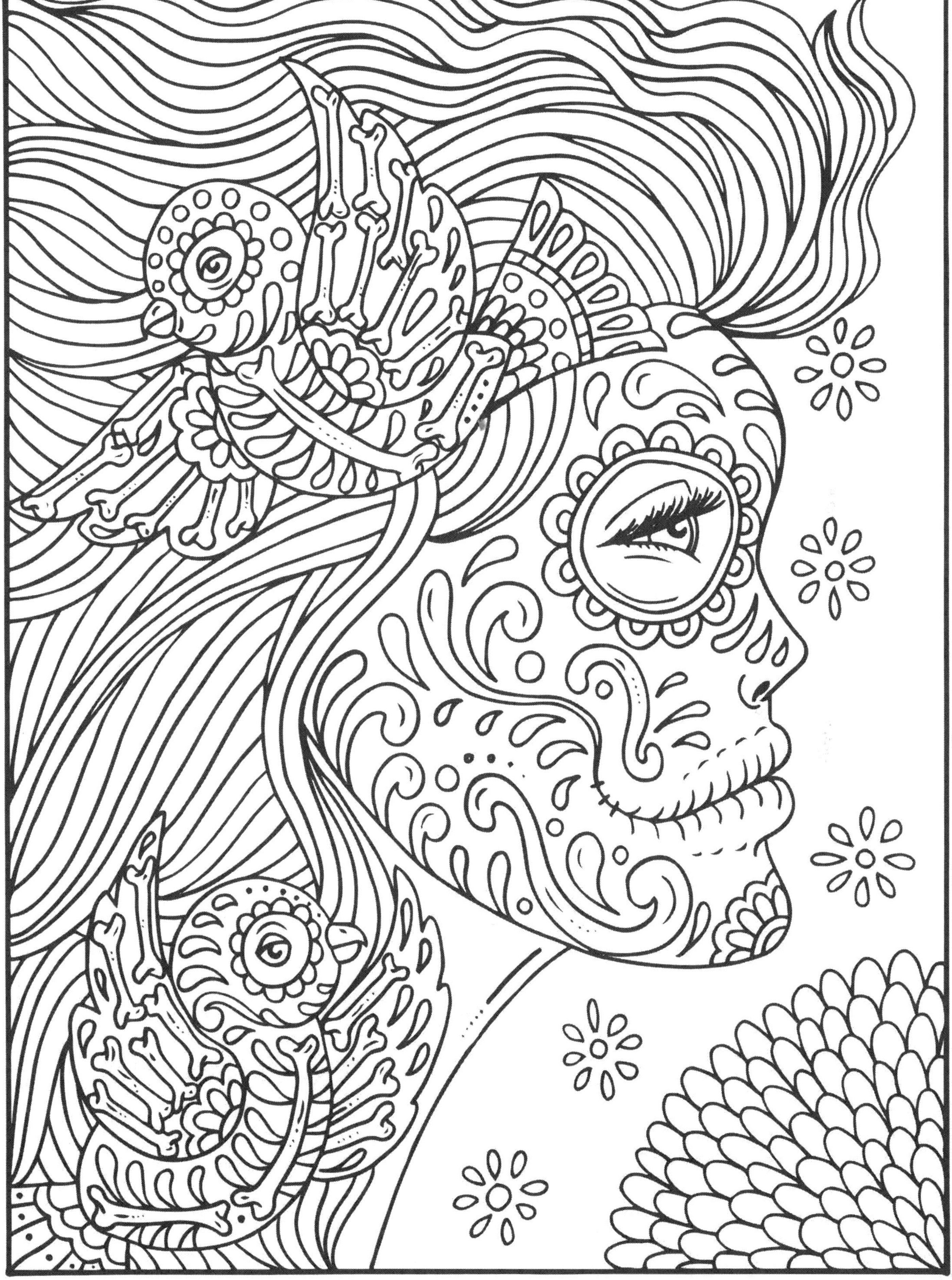

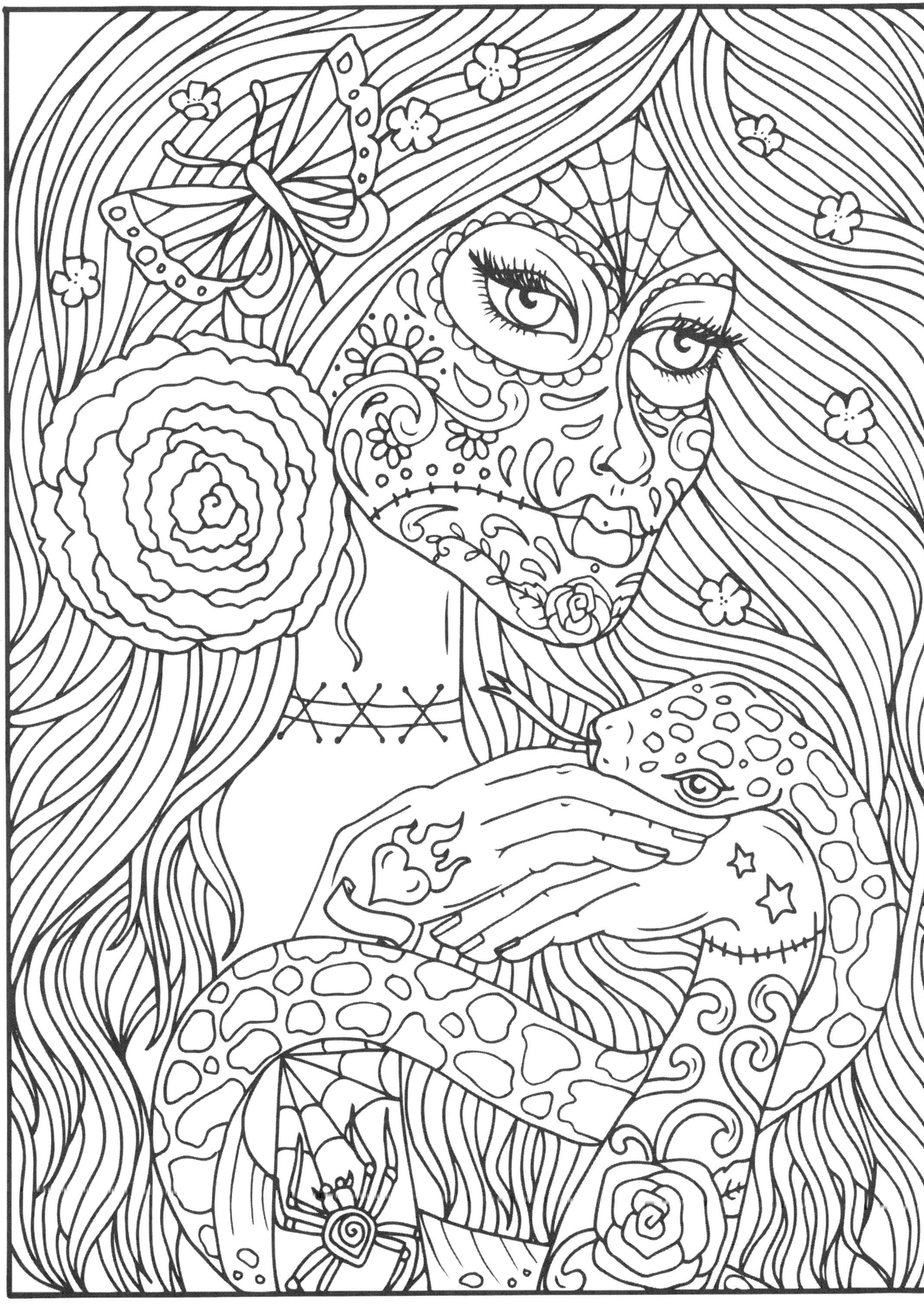

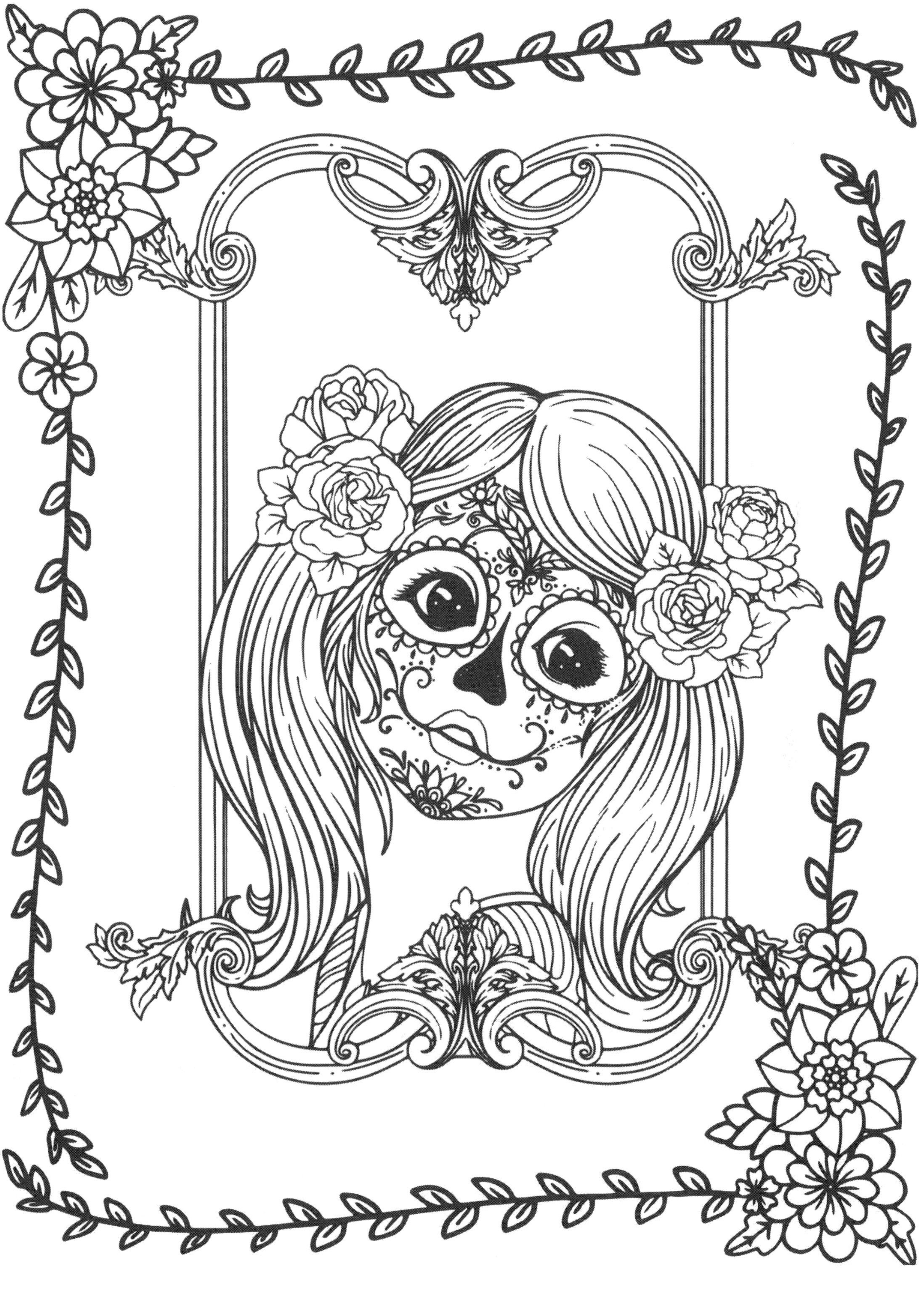

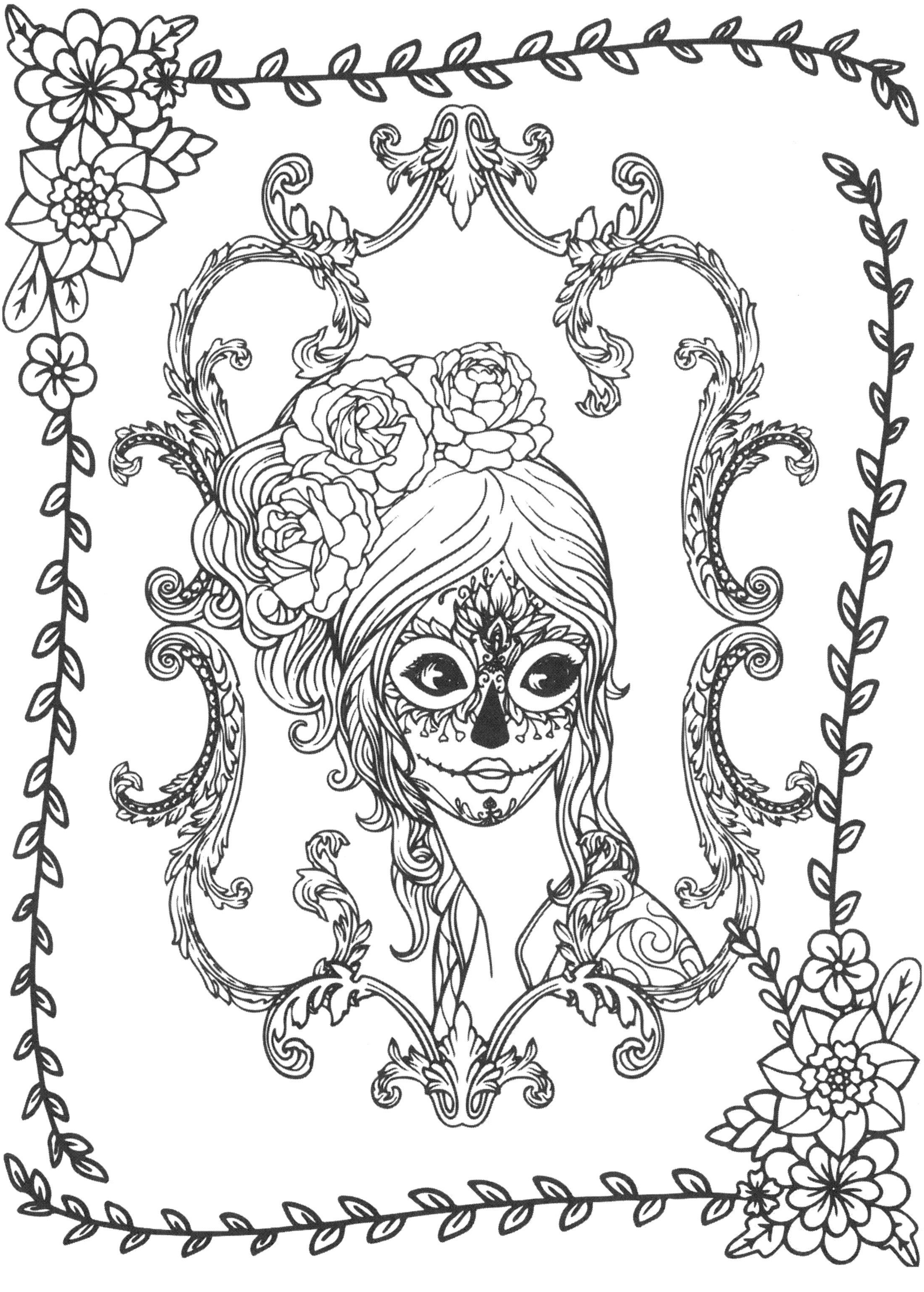

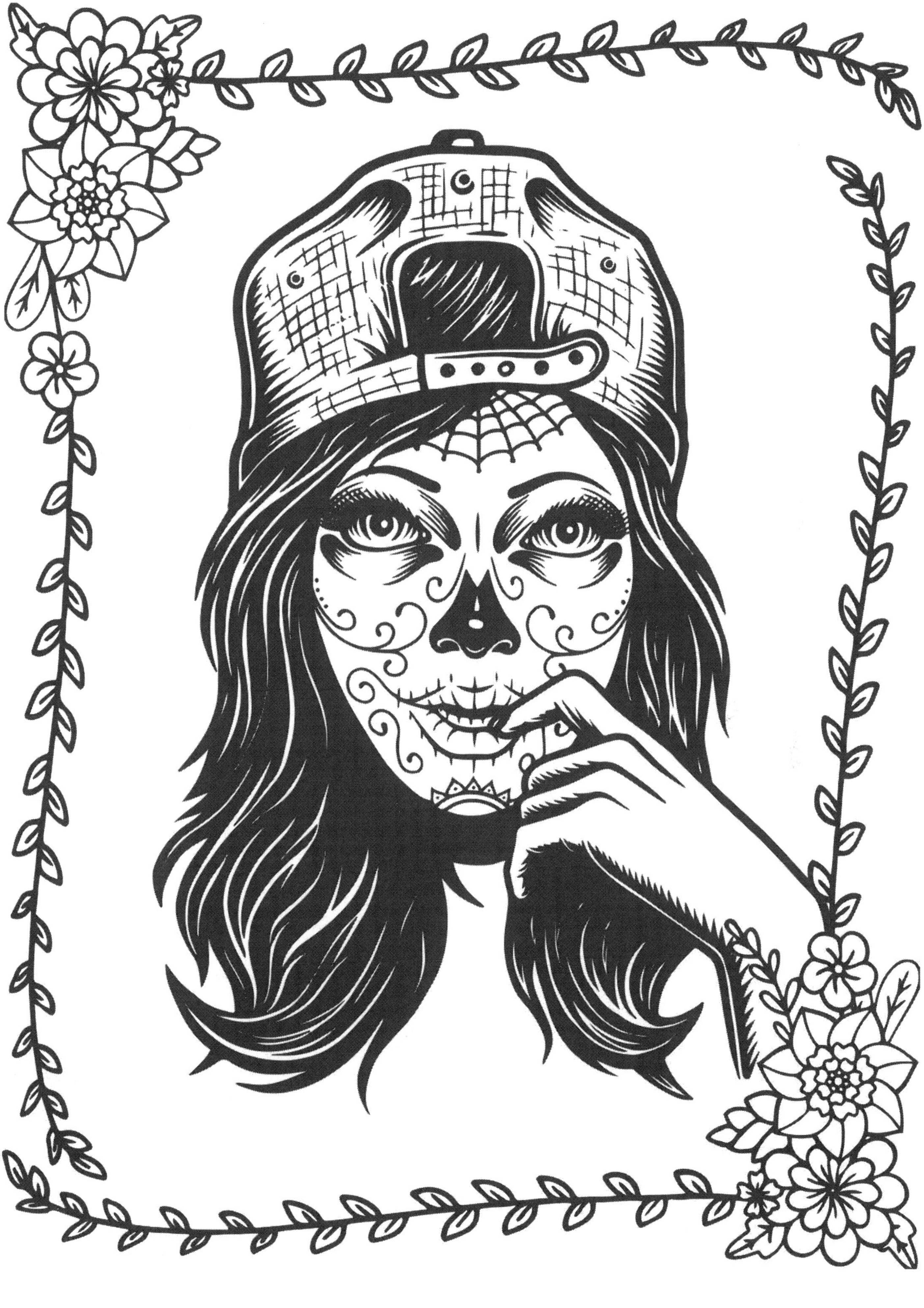

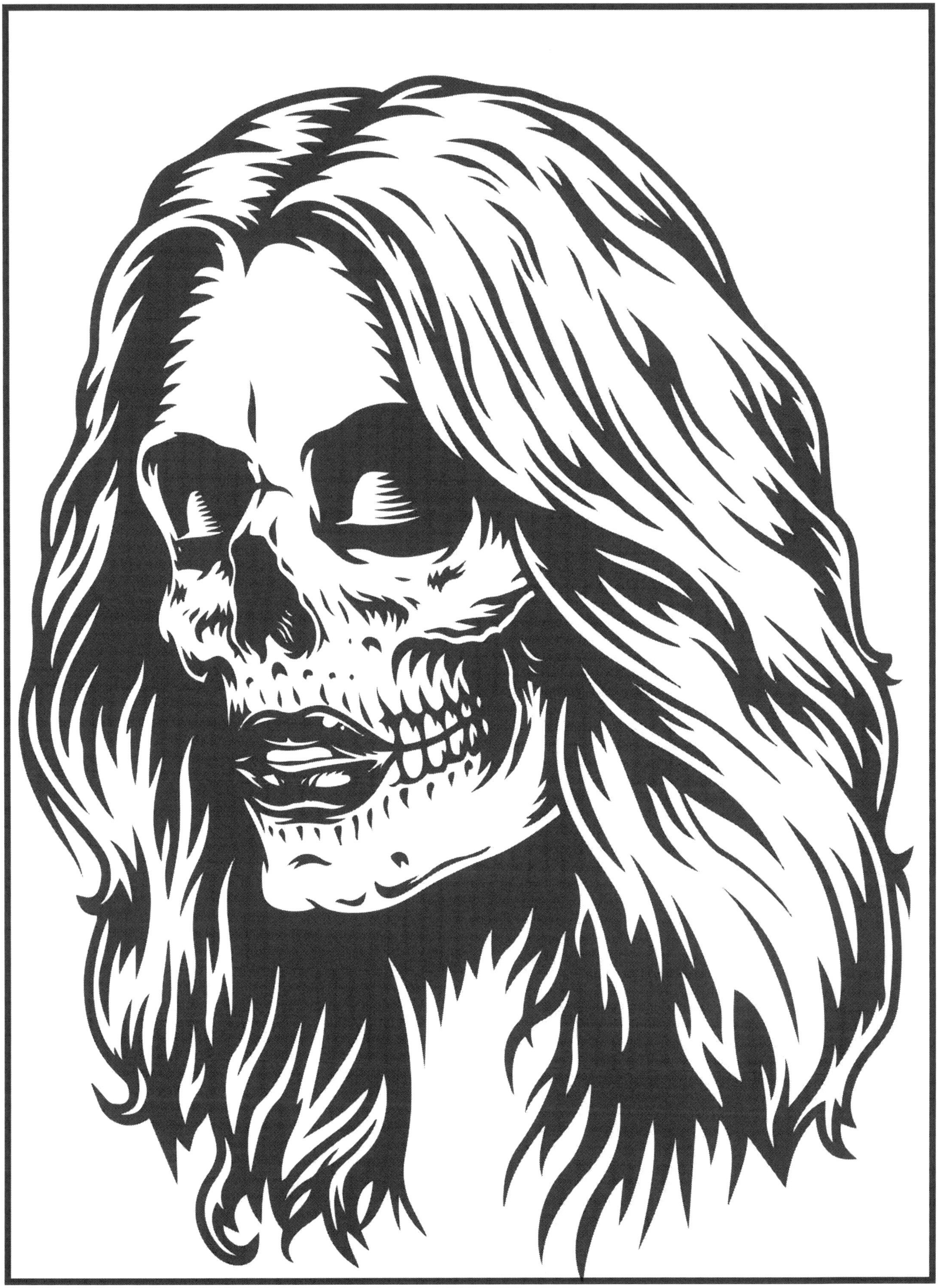

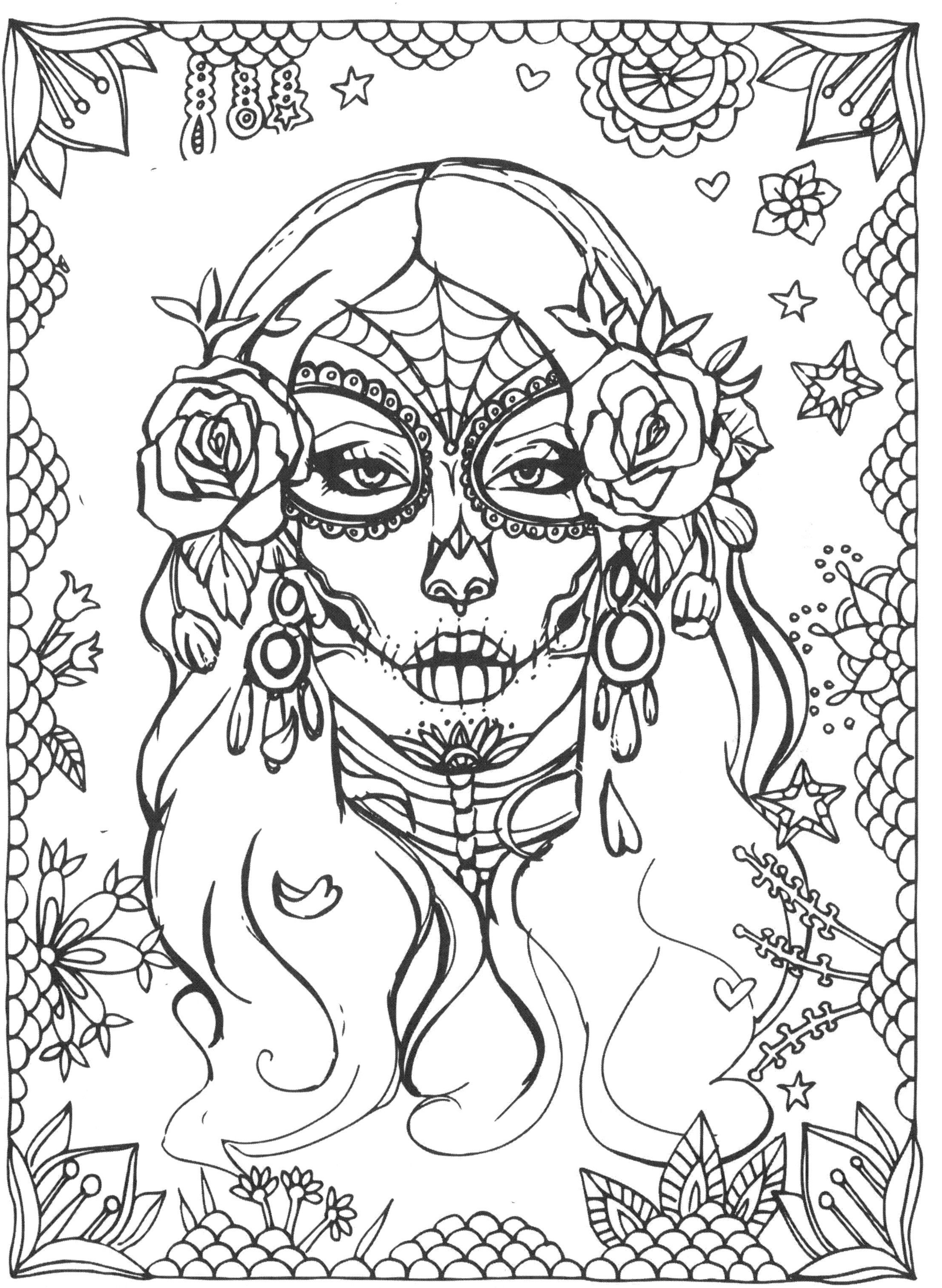

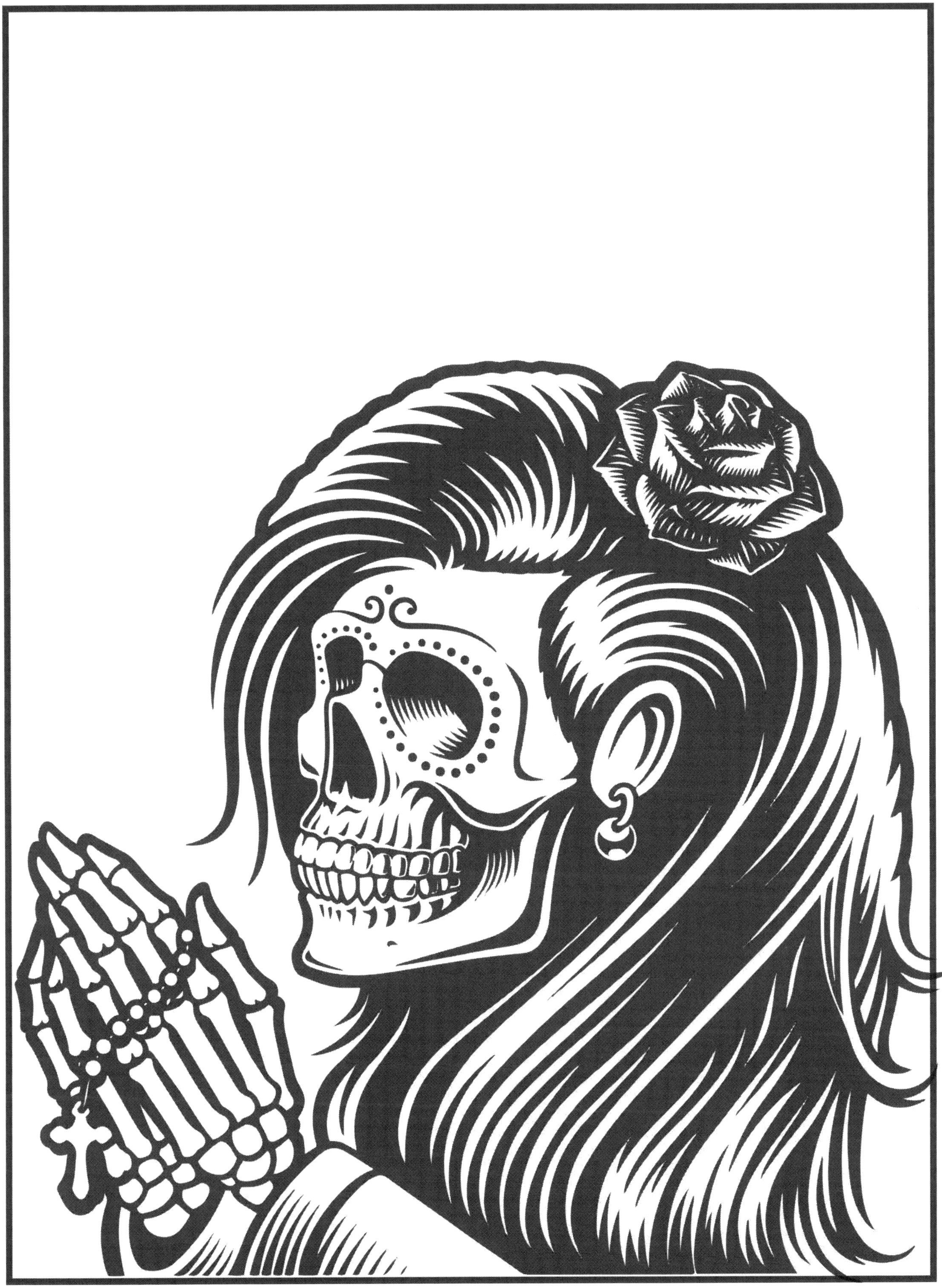

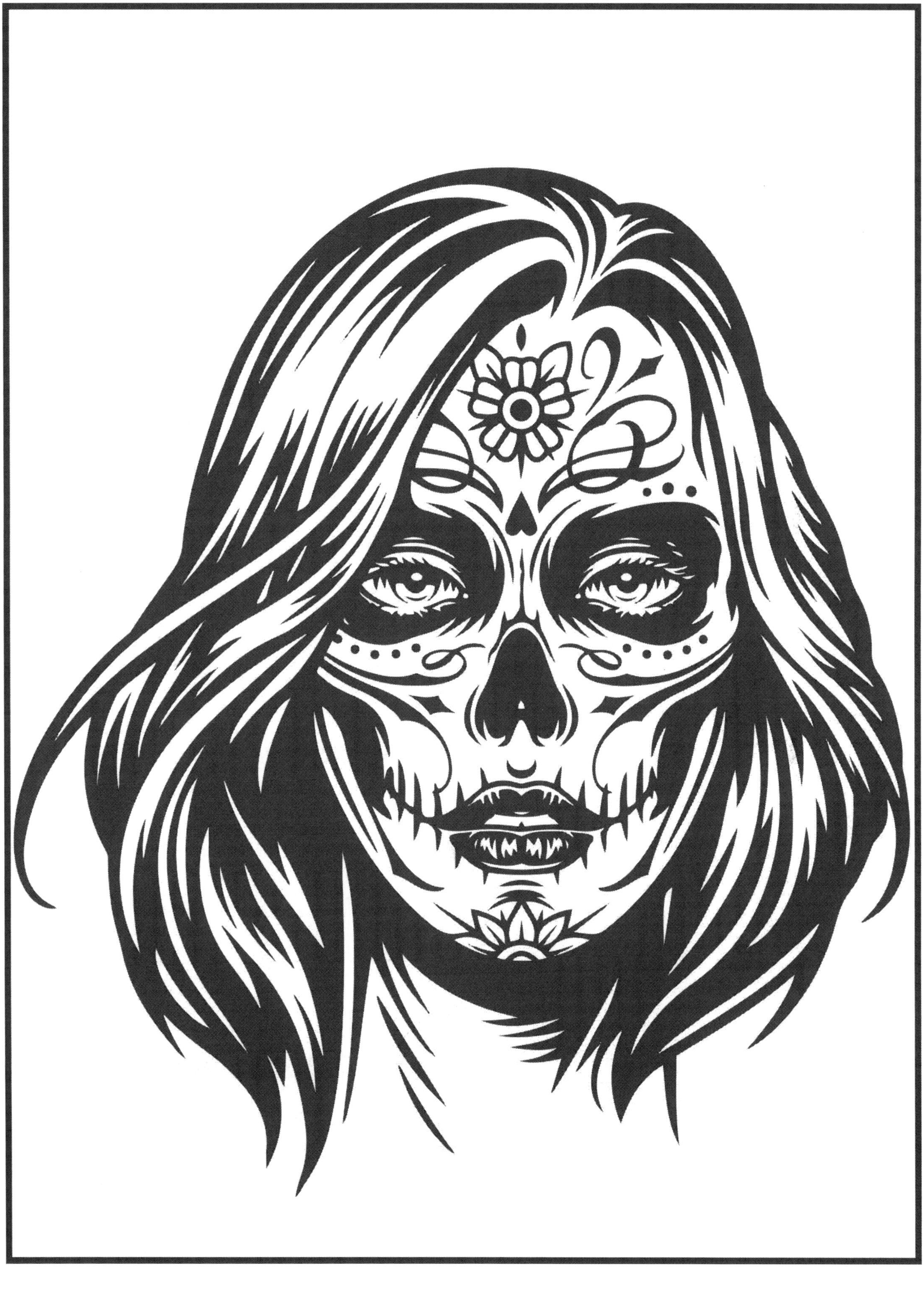

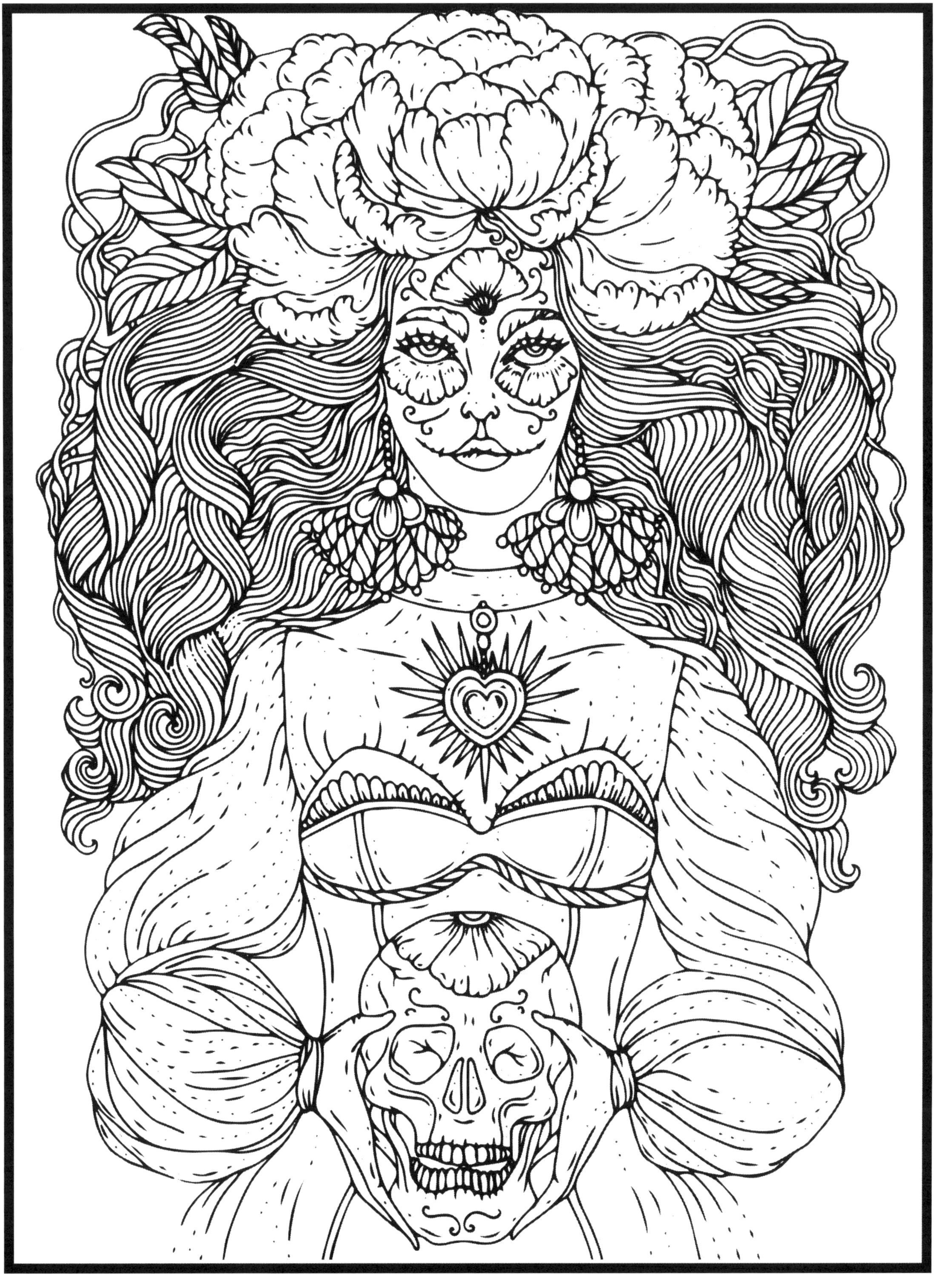

Made in United States
Orlando, FL
30 November 2021

10961758R00015